ISBN 978-1-63393-313-2

Pine House Publishing

In association with

◤ köehlerstudios™

"The Lagoon Princess"

© Copyright 2016 Jana Meador

All Rights Reserved. No part of this publication may be reproduced, stored in a retrieval system, or transmitted in any form or by any means – electronic, mechanical, photocopy, recording, or any other – except for brief quotations in printed reviews, without the prior written permission of the author.

About the Author

Jana Meador is a novelist and a dedicated animal advocate. She has helped many pets in need, including dogs, cats and birds.

Meador studied screenwriting at New York Film Academy. She is a two-time Honorable Mention in the Depth of Field International Film Festival and the finalist in the Alaska International Film Awards.

This is her fifth published book.
www.janameador.com

Front cover design and interior illustrations by Ian Welsh.
www.behance.net/vicariouspress

 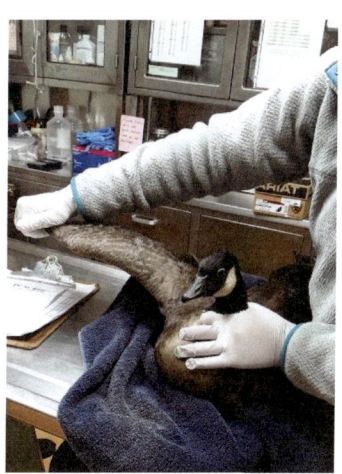 

This story is inspired by the rescue of a Canadian goose (Cackling variety), that took place on Westchester Lagoon in Anchorage, Alaska.

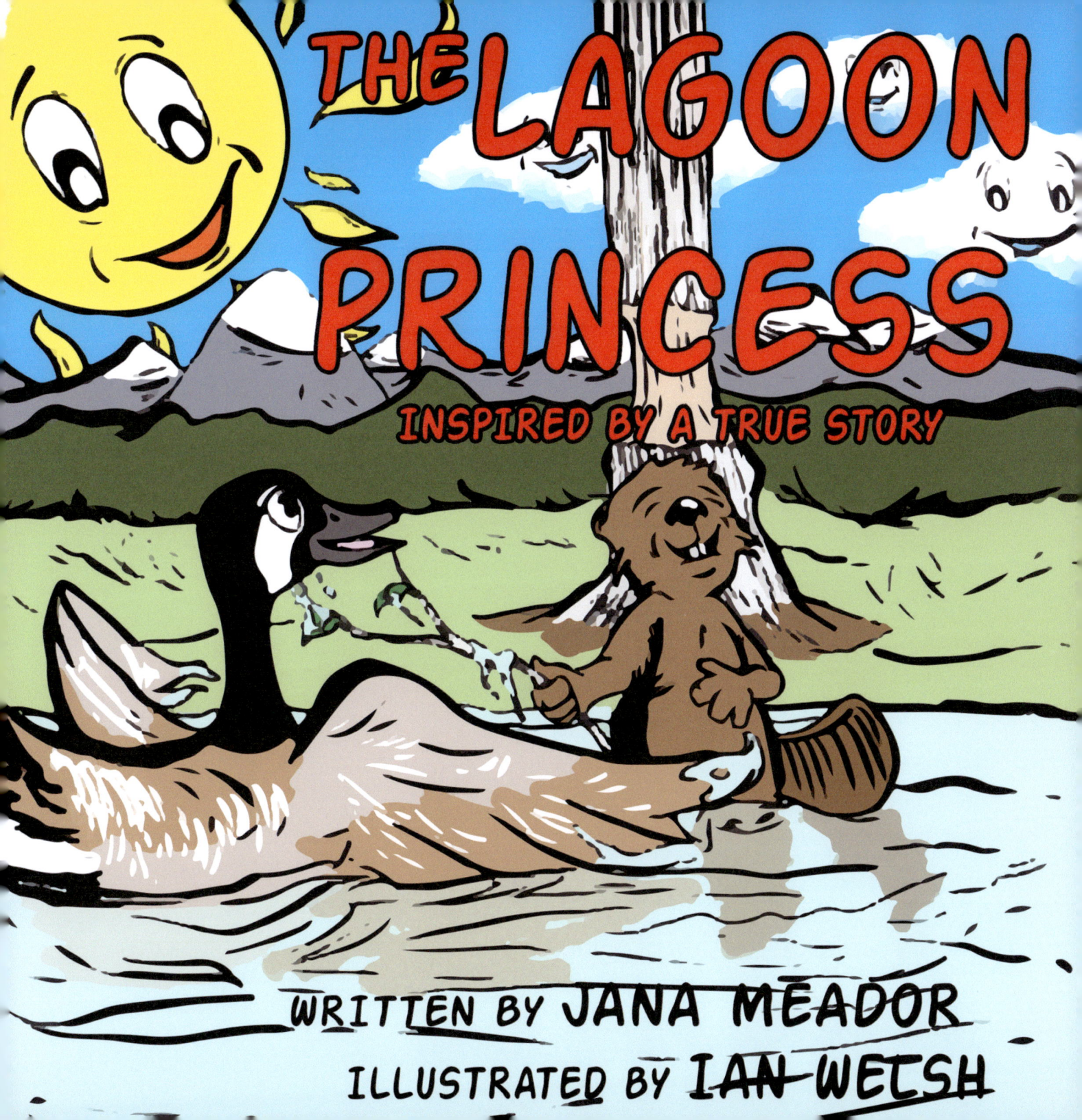

SPRING

The glittering sun covered the sweet water pond,

On the large lagoon by the bridge,

Where people crossed,

To see the many birds,

After the winter's snow and freeze, the lagoon came to life,

And welcomed birds with colorful feathers,

Webbed feet and pointed beaks,

Landing on the surface,

Moving the sun beams of the water into rolling waves and circles.

One of the feathered birds, Princess of the Lagoon, made many friends

With ducks, loons and swans,

Happily cruising through the lagoon's edge,

Her dark eyes glancing left and right –

She jumped onto the shore and rushed to green patch of grass,

She nibbled with her beak, her daily lunch, what a delicious treat!

When the outside light dimmed, and the dark, silky veil spread

Across the sky,

The stars proudly shined through,

Bright with their endless pillow of glittering starlets

The heavenly parade of lights,

Down below Princess rested her wings,

Folded by her shoulders, her feet in the blending pillow of

Luminous stars, that reflected on the lagoon's surface,

Princess quietly slept before the sunrise comes

And opens its curtain to another day, where she can joyfully play.

Happy and cheerful and full of life,

Our Princess paddled with her new friend and through the pond,

A beaver swimming next to her, rushing to the water's edge,

Where he climbed and headed to the tree

To sharpen his teeth –

The beaver took a smaller branch and splashed the Princess's head.

She stretched her neck and spread her wings

And flapped them on the water,

The beaver took off with the stolen branch

And down under the lagoon he quickly swam.

Princess goose walked on the grass,

With the sun warming up her feathers. She lowered her head to eat,

When a grasshopper jumped over her beak.

He hopped quickly over the grass, saying hello

To little geese hatches surrounded by their mama,

She rushed them to the water,

Today, they learned to follow her behind –

All the siblings swimming in a row, what a parade, what a joy!

Rain, rain, go away! Princess walked through mud,

She lifted her head, and stretched her neck and flapped her wings,

As she fought the wind,

Princess shook her feathers and bared the drops

She jumped through paddles and hopped to the nearest grassy crops.

A flock of geese landed on the water,

Princess hurried to joined them in,

Happy, she swam toward their king.

When an otter popped his head from above the water

Princess hissed, and the otter got scared, disappearing into the lake.

She told her stories to her friends, what she's seen and whom she's met

All the lagoon's secret tales.

There were shadows lurking at night

And dandelions came to bloom only

When the daylight spread across the sky.

There were eagles that flew above

And all the birds knew, to keep together,

To scare the eagles, two big birds,

Who flew away, hungry, perhaps for another day?

SUMMER

All the smells of wildflowers in the summer sun

Attracted big striped bumblebees that flew over having fun.

They landed on the fragrant blossoms,

Next to Princess and her friends,

In the warm, sunny day they all had a nice stay.

With yellow pollen on bumblebees' legs

Princess too, made herself useful,

And so with her pointed beak, she trimmed the grass

That grew around the lagoon and underneath her youthful feet.

A little boy screeched with joy,

When his small fingers,

Brushed softly over the loon's back, that lay in the sun.

The red-eyed bird got spooked,

And ran for the water,

When Princess jumped on the shore, and hissed at the schoolboy,

Who rushed to his mother's arms, his face beamed with joy.

The long summer days and the everlasting sun,

Made it a lot of fun,

To be at the lake –

The beaver and his bigger brother otter,

Came back and swam across,

To see what's new, and to greet all the little ones, who were born

And their feathered mothers,

Who taught their offspring to follow behind,

Even Princess watched

as the two-week old ducklings followed in a row, behind their mama's tow.

Happy to have so many friends,

Princess quickly swam,

Using her webbed feet,

Paddling through the lagoon's deepest inland sea.

There she passed two turtle twins,

Sun tanning on planking, floating wooden beam.

And there, closer to the shore,

Her beak touched the white petal lilies –

That grew up and toward the sun, in the summer's warmest month.

Dark cloud came and covered the sky,

And light rain drizzled down,

Princess told herself, "I'd better run,"

And so she hid in the tall bushy grass,

Surrounded by mallards, and another goose,

And there, they felt safe when the loud thunder came,

And rumbled grumpily over their beloved lagoon.

Our Princess turned her head

And quickly stuck her beak

Into her warm feathered back,

Waiting for the rain to go away.

AUTUMN

Princess heard the flock of geese from high above,

They flew in over the mountains' peaks.

She watched them as they flapped their wings,

Descending on the lagoon, the Canadian geese

Held their feathers wide apart, as their feet touched the water's part.

One, by one landed on the lake,

And surrounded Princess.

The geese washed dust from their wings –

They collected while they traveled the distance

To get where they are now –

Princess laughed to see them flap their wings,

And roll their bodies up and down,

Diving their heads –

They cleaned their wings and when they were done,

Rested peacefully and waited for the night.

On a late evening our Princess goose came upon two moose.

They stopped by the lagoon to eat the red apples - a delicious treat,

Princess walked under the baby moose's feet.

The mother sow flicked her ears as

Princess soaked her webbed feet to paddle

Away to leave the mama moose and her baby

To enjoy their sweet apple treat.

She swam across the lake and hid in a tall bushy trail

Princess tucked her feet to keep warm in the Alaskan autumn's fall.

Where did all that green grass go,

Princess wondered.

Hungry and cold she stood alone in rain and mud –

All her friends already left, heading south.

She tried the patch of yellow grass,

But didn't like it.

Hungry, she went to sleep.

Alone, in the dark, she dreamt of birds,

And bees, and colorful flowers,

Even the frogs made their way,

Into Princess's night sphere,

And little fish came too, tickling her webbed feet,

As she slept on the cold, autumn dark, watery sheet.

WINTER

White light pieces fell from the grey sky

Down on the ground and all around our Princess.

The fluffy flakes stayed on her back making her feathers wet.

"It's snow," the friendly duck had told her.

This was the first time Princess heard that snow comes down

And upon the earth from the sky.

"For how long will it snow?" Princess wanted to know.

In the morning the nature changed into a white blanket –

A winter's tale.

Princess woke up with her wings deep in snow,

And some frost on her chest that she cleaned with her beak.

Oh so cold, she shivered from the bottom of her feet.

The lagoon now covered with ice, she slid across

When she heard young kid's voice.

Princess hurried over the frozen lake,

But the kids didn't have food –

They carried skates and headed away on another lake.

As the boys and girls crossed the bridge,

One noticed the lonely goose surrounded by a snowy field.

The little girl worried a bit, she slid her hand into her warm jacket,

Taking out her sandwich, she said, "Eat," and hungry Princess quickly snatched, the little

Pieces of the delicious bread.

The light outside did not last long. The darkness and cold

Is that what she was told –

The winter meant in the Alaskan cold?

Sometimes the ducks flew back to say hi,

To their only Canadian goose friend at this time of the year,

The rest of the geese enjoyed their winter treat somewhere far away, in southern heat.

Princess felt weak trying to keep some heat,

By standing on one foot while she hid the other,

Under her broken feathered wing.

The nature so white but bitterly cold,

And quiet –

Princess dreamt of green grass and friends she had met

She hoped to see the otter and the red-eyed loons,

And the majestic swans

That used to accompany her on the lagoon.

The kids came back for her,

The place dark and windy,

More snow fell down on ground, when

They threw cracked corn close to her beak.

She stretched her neck and quickly ate,

This delicious, nutritious treat.

Princess waited for them every single day –

That's how she was able to survive her lonely stay.

The corn kept her belly full and happy,

She no longer hissed at any kids.

One day, some adults came,

Taking our Princess away.

She found a new place, warm and full of light –

She didn't have to freeze her webbed feet

Not for another night!

Who were these strangers? She didn't know.

But she enjoyed her green salad and more corn.

They even made the tiniest pond

She had ever seen,

They placed her in, and she would swim

Happy to have water underneath her feathered wings.

Gentle, soft hands touched Princess's wing

Stretching it to the side to see,

If the damage can be fixed,

So the bird could fly again and join her friends.

And every day, Princess found a way, to work hard

With her human friend –

To let the girl, who cared for her,

Move her wing, slowly and carefully,

Hoping that next spring our Princess will

Join a new flock of her beloved feathered geese,

On her lagoon, she longed to be released.

What a surprise when she heard,

The boy's and girl's happy, familiar voices,

They came to visit her to her new, indoor home.

She hissed to make them laugh,

And the girl handed her the fresh green salad knowing,

Princess would chew it quickly,

Begging for more, the boy and the girl, were glad to see,

Their Princess growing stronger,

She got along, with everyone in her rescue home.

Roaming freely to her own pool, or going outdoors,

Princess could do all that, and more!

ANOTHER YEAR, ANOTHER SPRING...

After long winter months of receiving the proper care,

The veterinarian smiled and said,

"The Princess is good to go" –

She should strive and live happily ever after

In her new outdoor home.

Soon after they took her in a crate,

To release her back, to lagoon in the spring's warm air.

So happy and full of life,

Princess swam among her friends,

All the loons, and ducks and swans

They returned back to their summer home.

The kids were there, saying hello,

And smiling,

Their Princess found her Prince!

He flew from far away, on that beautiful spring day.

Keeping close to her,

Our Princess was no longer alone!

Prince so proud to have his Princess by his side,

He promised, he won't ever leave her,

He will not go anywhere, without his feathered love!

Prince challenged her to fly, to stretch her wings

They took toward the sunny sky!

The kids, the boy and the girl, watched from the ground,

As the pair of geese happily flew, one next to another

To enjoy the day and time, they forever shared together.

THE END

Printed by Libri Plureos GmbH in Hamburg, Germany